Rules for Rearrangement

Poems by
Julie Babcock

Glass Lyre Press

Copyright © 2020 Julie Babcock
Paperback ISBN: 978-1-941783-71-9

All rights reserved: Except for the purpose of quoting brief passages for review, no part of this book may be reproduced or transmitted in any form or by any means, electronic or mechanical, including photocopying, recording, or by any information storage and retrieval system, without permission in writing from the publisher.

Design & Layout: Steven Asmussen
Cover Art: © Roberto Maggioni | Dreamstime.com
Copyediting: Linda E. Kim

Glass Lyre Press, LLC
P.O. Box 2693
Glenview, IL 60025
www.GlassLyrePress.com

Rules for Rearrangement

Praise for *Rules for Rearrangement*

My people believe in thin places that exist between this world and the next. It is there we can hear our dead. Julie Babcock has sentenced a book so between genre, it exists as if between these worlds. Wrought in response to the sudden death of her husband, she collages aphorisms, tiny slippages of language, irreverent quips, fragments of prose, and "gathers the shards and makes songs." In a time of great public despair, this is a book that sings and singes grief, to keep us going on, one that can guide us all, back and forth across the veil.

—Sean Thomas Dougherty, *author of The Second O of Sorrow*

In *Rules for Rearrangement* Babcock describes life after death through videogames, fairy tales, science fiction, esoteric jokes. As she runs red lights and jackhammers, makes enchiladas, moves through days that just keep coming, Babcock defamiliarizes the defamiliarizing effects of living with grief with a heartachingly generous lightness and wit. And the impact is rattling--she makes poetry cave-paint and conjure again, bringing back into being both her beloved, and our attention to the vulnerability of our bonds and bodies.

—Megan Levad, *author of What Have I to Say to You*

"All things break and fall against this life,/and this life gathers the shards and makes song," Julie Babcock writes in this dazzling poetry/hybrid collection. Here, the gaps, ellipses, and erasures are like the clefts across which synapses fire. The cleft is between life and death, and the fire comes from Babcock's language and fearless structure. This book is a song, a fugue, a state of both being and becoming – and it will rearrange your mental furniture."

—Sue William Silverman, *author of If the Girl Never Learns*

Contents

The News	1
Messengers	5
Diplomats	17
Arson	29
Guide	39
Warps	61
Acknowledgements	75
About the Author	77

The News

"He's dead," they said. "Do you have anyone we can call?"

Messengers

There are too many messengers.
Sometimes, a husband and wife

do not part. They return from work together.
Imagine February snow in her hair and his hand

and their breath framing a nearing house. Or
she pushes police from her kitchen so hard

her hands become walls.
She kneels and her body becomes the floor.

Her heart becomes stone. Her fingers
become the phone she presses to make the first call to God.

No, she begins, even before he answers.

She zips her coat on the porch the realtor said was perfect
for lemonade and magnolia blossoms.

In this other season, several branches
snap under the weight of sudden snow.

It is a long driveway and her weariness is deep.
The shovel sinks in and she clears what she can

but the difference she makes is too small.

She could defrost something. All those beautiful tomatoes she roasted when she cooked for two. Begun from heirloom seeds she watered until bursting. Transplanted to homes big enough for growth. Each root tucked into black gold soil. Supported and taught to climb cages. The whole summer dotted with small, yellow flowers. And then deep purple beefsteaks she sliced and drizzled with oil. 400 degrees forever until the air thickened with pulp.

"We'll eat them all winter," she thought.

Everyone has choices
and is represented by choices—

    —as long as you don't try and talk to the stone.

CEMETARY OFFICER: We can carve anything. Whatever he liked. Whatever you want

VINYL BINDER: We have photocopied vines and hearts. Angels and insignias

TISSUE: There's more in this box

GRASS: I'm underneath this snow. Once the temperatures warm, my roots will unfreeze and I'll grow again

WIND: I can sting your neck, your lips, your fingers. Anything you expose

PLASTIC BAG: I have your husband's ring and phone

THE STONE: Nothing will change this

She returns to work to teach students   why they need her
    though she knows less than before   without answers to questions
and can't recall the long room number   she tried to write on her hand
                    the black tip   too intimate and wet

She draws boxes on the
blackboard to show how
one thing moves into
another.

A couch into a room. A
grave into snow.

                                    Or is it snow into a grave?

His   thick,
windswept   hair
doesn't fit inside.

She watches assassin movies   as snow continues
                from bed   after-death blankets
which do not warm her   his scarf
               no heat   his sweater
while *Nikita* retrains   her skin
        her instincts   her hope
in a shining restaurant   a small box
           with a gun   instead of jewelry
      and an extra clip   against a bricked-in window

She is told to write a Valentine from the dead. What he would say to her if he was alive. No. What he would say dead like he is but able to send a message.

She sits at the grief support table and chooses a pair of scissors. She cuts and glues two hearts together—one from red paper, the other from white.

Words come small and true. Words they only spoke to each other when the whole world was nothing but them. Nothing but their scrap of paper nonsense and names.

the hearts begin to beat

She is told to write a Valentine to the dead. What she would say to him if he was alive.
    No. What she would say to him dead like he is but able to receive a message.

Every day she tries to get it right. She is ashamed of her anger and this writing going on and
    on about her. When they first met, he handed her

a glass of water. The chip in the rim. Why he reached out to touch her lips. When they first
    met, he wrote a poem. *My days are dogs*

that don't come when I call. They met, and he took photographs of her red car as it aged. He
    didn't like change. He didn't like it

when a thunderstorm blew out the electricity. Every day she isn't trying hard enough. She
    wants to say she loves him. She wants her message pure

                                                a flashlight and a whistle

Curious, how when she shakes the box there is no noise, just hollow weight. With index finger and thumb on either side, she pulls the green ribbon out straight, moves it aside and lifts.

It is empty. She silences the phone, locks the door, and tries to fill it. All day she brings things to the box: her apple, loose change, photographs, the wedding ring. But each time something touches the bottom, it disappears. She keeps trying. She loses Tuesday and Thursday and her own birthday replacing emptiness with books and pillows and coffee cups. She hoists in a 50-pound bag of cat litter and then the two cats. When she is the only thing left, she lifts one foot in, and then the other.

Diplomats

She unfolds the paper in this dark country. Her mission: to find the masked outlaw with a black cape who fights against tyranny. They met in a candlelit church.

The prisoner planning his escape. The idea of her keeps him focused. Every day, another teaspoonful of dirt.

The cowboy on the free range. When her horse reared at the edge of a Colorado River canyon, he grabbed her just in time.

The mayfly who lives less than an hour.

The man who hides bills in the closet.

The star who lives 10 billion years and becomes a super nova

The lover who still carries her scent.

The locked door. She scours the region for the key.

An alien lands in the middle of the town square where you were born. He carries a laser gun or a telekinetic device that makes the future uncertain. His set of demands includes a siphon for the ocean, all the olive branches, and the children.

How is work? How is life? How do you go on?

Everyone is curious
about life after death.
Everyone is
frightened and wants
reassurance
          If she can avoid
          crawling under
          she will have
          answered enough.

                The immoveable restaurant table

      To drink is to pay
      attention to glass.

                 Everyone will
                 feel better if she
                 sips the gin
                 slowly.

                    Time is running
Because he died

                    The strapless watch

                    They say hello, nice to see you
Because he died

                    On the ambulance street

                    She is talking to students
Because he died

                    Making photoessay dedications

                                        She needs to write

                                        So tired the words are boxes

The shadow demands another piggyback ride

PASSERBY: What's weighing you down?
SHE: Don't you see it?
PASSERBY: See what?
SHE: Wait a minute, I need to sit down

Everyone is filled with a heavy combination
of blockage and sun.

THE SUN: I was formed from a gravitational collapse and have not changed dramatically in four billion years

THE SHADOW: Giddy-Up

Leave, she repeats. The cough inside her is a little ball. Then she realizes
 a ball cannot hear. A boy must accompany the ball.

Please, she tells the child, take this ball away. I can't reach it. The boy is
young and nimble. He could easily zoom down the hallway

and kick it elsewhere. She keeps the light on, hoping. Little boy,
can you hear me? She is stuck inside her body's flimsy walls. She knows

he is a very busy child. He might be crawling through a tunnel or floating in a bath.
The hall closet is filled

with thousands of toys. He might be lining them up from door to door.

All
words are nailed
to antonyms she thinks as she listens
to machines building a garage next door. She is surrounded
by pillows and books, shape-changing casings
so quiet she moves to check they exist. It is almost Christmas
again she thinks trying not to think of death. The neighbors will have
a new house for their car. She will travel to family and stop herself from crying
when they serve dinner. She will be grateful. She will hide her box of nails
and kneel under
the happiness tree.

Once there was a woman who wanted to belong. She lived on a paper boat outside the book and every morning she sailed to its pages, dropped anchor, and pried it open. When it grew too dark to read she drifted through the sea with the flying fish and stars. Everything glistened and the waves rolled without breaking. She slept and dreamt in buoyancy.

Each morning the book got heavier until one day she couldn't get it open. She stretched across the cover. Sun dried salt into crystals on her spine.

When planning your own birthday party, it is important to distribute the invitations at the right time. Older invitees take longer to make decisions. Take a buzzfeed quiz to determine your age.

Or just hand out the invitations and wait. If no one responds, you can skip the buzzfeed quiz. Order a big cake regardless. You don't want to be remembered for letting your old friends go hungry.

Think about utensils. Nothing ever stays in the same place and everything must be moved from one location to another. Small boxes and place settings. Once at your parent's table. Once with your husband. Now with yourself.

When you go to bed and dream you are falling off a cliff, hold the crumbling edge and remember that this is only a dream. That you aren't dead—   The swift air separates

    a plate of ground

               layers and candles

Arson

The long
fabric of
shirts and
the
shoulders
of
hangers.

                                                      She stands under
                                                      his closet light and
                                                      feels the heat from
                                                      his body.

                              His fleece pullover softer
                              than ash.

                              The blaze in the furnace

It is a small car and a large wall. The distance isn't much. Think about the accelerator and the brake. Two side-by-side parts pushed down by the same thing. She still feels his hand touching her back even though they say it is gone.

If one thing is separated from another for too long they can never return the same. The curves of space are unstable. She says, I miss you, and off pops the side mirror. Now there's a hole that sounds push through when she drives fast. Now there's a hole whether she drives straight in or swerves to park.

The police issue her a speeding ticket. And then another. And then they bring a cyclops along and charge her for running a red light at night.

OFFICER: Whoa. You just blew through that light. What are you doing?

WHITE CAMRY: We are running from death

OFFICER: License and registration

GLOVE COMPARTMENT: I have the registration tucked somewhere in all the maps of places she went with her beloved

OFFICER: Where are you going?

WHITE CAMRY: On an odyssey

GLOVE COMPARTMENT: I have the receipts for that too

OFFICER: *shines his flashlight into her eyes*

GLOVE COMPARTMENT: Have you stopped to consider what happens when you ask her to open me? I'm trying to hold private things in the dark until they bind together. The certificate of my birth. A secret note on a napkin. Souvenir matchbooks. Instructions to regions filled with song. When you ask her to open the compartment, we risk loss. We already lost for the first officer and then, before we could regroup, for the second officer. Something always falls out in the process. Something is always thrown away. Why can't you leave us alone in this dark? What are you hoping to prove accosting us with your unbearably bright cyclops eye?

THE CYCLOPS: I like you. I will eat you last

She has a kingdom and a sword because there are so many battles and the wood is bewitched. She fights better when there's something to protect—children and dogs and ideas—a whole fortress of good feeling and strong stone. When an alarm sounds, she takes down the blade that hangs over her bed and goes through the gate alone because every lost second is another binding of the enemy's spell: *You will lose sight. You will lose purpose. You will lose love.* The trees hang whatever they catch. So many of her cloaks already choked in the tallest limbs. The earth opens its mouth whenever there is trembling. But. She is good at jumping.

    Her sword slices through another monster.

Everyone laughed and complimented her
on another good joke.

IONESCO: I mean, a bear. I wasn't expecting something with such large claws
BECKETT: I'm going to wait under this tree until the Gryphon comes
SISYPHUS: Keep pouring on the antiseptic!

Last week she brought in a snake pit for the guests and the week before that a hornets' nest. She said she wanted to be alone

THE BEAR: RAAAWWWRRR!

Hahahahaha

To remove concrete, first determine whether you need a jackhammer or whether a
    little drill will do. How much was poured? How far does it go down?

Break up the big slab into little slabs. This takes a long time and involves your tool
    of choice and an additional hard rubber mallet. Keep going long after your
    fingers and arms become numb. Imagine you are opening a vault.

Inside this vault is an elixir that ensures you will never die nor your children nor
    anyone you love. It smells like the grass after a rain and was carried into
    the vault by Walt Whitman who rubbed it all over his body and in this
    way made more.

Let your boot-soles sink into the grass. Throw yourself upon the crowbar and pry
    away the lifeless pieces. The spreading elixir. The vault spilling into itself.
    Your ringing arms. Your shooting spine. Drop to your knees and call
    into this uncovered darkness. All these uncovered sisters and brothers.
    Nematodes flashing like veins of gold. Pockets of chrysalis pulsing open.
    Riches in root fingers and the protection of particles that receive and
    awaken.

                                      —all grows and grows together.

Introduce your new self and explain your need. For instance: I need rules for rearrangement. For instance: I need to box memories. I need to let my objects know it's not them.

Rearrangement involves more than just one variable. The guitar from the chair and at different times of day when the sun opens and closes its boxes across the planks.

Empty space you uncover will be awkward and shy. Swab it clean and assure: I see you. You are here and welcome. I am sorry you had to hide. I am sorry you missed the sun, the wind, and music.

Former free space you cover will be angry. It will warp the planks until you trip. It will tilt and spill your drinks. Drop frames until they shatter. There is nothing you can do to soothe it. Look past the mutinies and never yield. You rearrange to survive. That hurricane and then you. The new Captain and Commander of Sacrifice.

Guide

You are here. You cannot fully explain.

This guide consists of many guides. You may choose to travel sequentially, or you may choose to travel by alternative algorithms. I am only here to keep you company. When you find yourself tired, take care to lie down and rest and I will rest with you.

i

You don't have the right shoes. You don't have the right weather. You chose to stay where you are, inside the home, inside the kitchen. You're about to close this guide.

You've been working on filling tortillas, rolling them up, placing them in a pan so they keep the shape you've given them. When a tortilla rips, you cover it with more sauce and cheese. Twelve fit in the pan that goes into the oven until the cheese melts and the flavors meld. You expect someone to arrive by the time this happens. You expect they will be there to wrap their arms around your waist as you pull your work from the oven and that they can save you from fire.

Then a shadow falls across the table and reveals a different universe. The sphere of one plate. A fork's prongs. The knife's horizon.

I'm sorry. I don't want to terrify.

ii

        Rocky Ford

            generosity

        down   water   lies

                       a woman

                                        almost

                                                    an island.

    The water deepens   before   and after

iii

A young woman moved to Indiana and was given this guide. She took it to a
    coffeehouse poetry reading where she met her late husband. She thought
    some of his poems were pretty good and that he was taller than any other
    man she'd ever dated. They went to the Knickerbocker and got drinks. She
    showed him this guide and they carried it through Indiana together. They
    found a house. They found a kitten. The last line of his last poem: *My days
    are dogs that don't come when I call.*

iv

We have been travelling for some time when you see a tree full of pomegranates. "Should we pick one?" you ask, but I cannot answer that. I am only here to keep you company. You consult this guide. This guide says pomegranates are a superfood.

We pick one and open it together. There, the impossibly red arils of juice, the meandering tributaries of white membranes—

                                                  an earth cracked open.

v

Hort Park

managed   by

                              a terrific place.

                                                    Open meadow

                                    Joy

        where you can   forget

                        We heard wood thrushes

vi

She married him here at the Tippecanoe Battlefield, the site of a deadly clash between white settlers and several Native American tribes because the depot was already booked and this site had a lovely white clapboard chapel and connected to a Heritage Trail. Her gown was simple and white, and she wore a clustered pearl veil in her upswept hair.

It was a hot July day, even the rehearsal the night before was hot. The girls stood over the vents in the floor letting the cooler air flow beneath their dresses. Only when ten years into the marriage, when her husband has a heart attack and dies, does it occur to her how much she doesn't know about his experience. All those days they stood without seeing each other. That morning of the wedding when they waited in separate rooms until the organist played and her dad walked her down the long aisle.

Near the chapel is the stone where the Prophet spoke to his ill-fated warriors almost 200 hundred years before. She was thinking about how many people are involved in a marriage and that they'd always be there. They were thinking they could stop General Harrison.

vii

Maybe you are not really here, you think. I do not argue. I brush your hair and
    check your buttons. You remember that you were just in the kitchen
    making enchiladas and that someone loved you.

I want to take away your grief. I kiss your cheek. I pull you toward me and hold
    you tight. Our faces are so close we share breath.

I used to be happy, you say, slamming me down to the riverbank.

viii

~~Happy~~ Hollow

        playground,

and   and

                nice   walk

                          (~~Good~~

                                                winter

places above

ix

We can move from one realm to another as soon as you realize.   doorways, crossroads, thresholds. Close   and visualize: wooden window shutters overgrown   ariel

We pass a three-way full-length   and you stop to look at yourself, slowly turning from one image to another. I think you are starting to understand

Then you grab   and shatter

x

██████████████████████████████████. Walls, █████
█████████████your eyes ████████████████████
█████. Ivy has █████

████████████████████mirror █████████████
███████one image ██████████████████████
█████████ a rock ████████each face

xi

Hearts quit all the time. That's what the glass box in the hallway is for. The defibrillator steps in when a body needs to send a message from one point to another, and can't make its own electricity. The defibrillator opens a cell gate.

Surprise! Electricity says. *You are the gates of the body, and you are the gates of the soul.*

You can open so many gates. The defibrillator says don't think of iron bar gates like the Debtor's Prison the government reopened in Alabama for people who can't escape poverty. Don't think of Newgate where people rotted before execution. Think of your favorite childhood gate, a small wooden one that doesn't weigh down like iron. That doesn't need a key, that doesn't even need your whole hand to lift and swing open.

Gates open and your brain sees a large group of people. Gates open and you kiss someone. Gates open and you fall in love. Gates open and send a message to your heart to contract. Again. The message is contract. Again. The message—

sing the body electric

xii

When it is too dark to see the flowers are at our feet, we should sleep.

xiii

The Monitor Canoe Trips people rent you a canoe

~~I'm not going to paddle, you tell me~~

~~I'm going to stay in this hell~~

The river runs fairly rapidly so the canoes are rather self-propelled

xiv

Jasper-Pulaski

                                                                                       an

every year

                pilgrimage.

                                                                                                             sometimes 40,000

                              then the land opens up

xv

You wake and stretch and crack open in every direction. Breath enters your
    spine and your arms pull you beyond. The bed. The floor. The house—

The land changes. Every day. What you used to have is gone. Every day. You walk
    through grief and fear to an 80-year-old agave plant in a greenhouse. The
    roof isn't high enough for the plant to unfurl its once-in-a-lifetime bloom.
    Not until you raise it.

xvi

We return to this kitchen table, and you offer me a fork. You say we've traveled
 a long way and we need to eat. You brush my hair away from my face
 and check my buttons. Somewhere, you tell me, in some lonely universe,
 people are taking pictures of their food.

We are not here to take photographs, you say, closing this guide. We are too awake
 and hungry.

Warps

Nothing better than to be alive and open-mouthed. She is remembering/learning.
    Her fingers spread across another's jaw, the hinged bones, the back and forth

kisses that keep seeking. Peaches she tasted as a girl. One bite out of each until all
    the bushels were tested. The mother who opened the basement door

to discover the change in harvest, who could not convince her of her crime, who
    made punishments as peach juice lingered on her tongue.

He smells like leaves, every glossy surface filled with veins. Ripe
                                                                  blushing skin.

Anything can get in or out when the door falls off its hinges.
Burrowing squirrels, song birds and stray cats. Even a curious person

wondering if they should still knock. Without a barricade,
cold wind visits the kitchen and hovers by the stove waiting

for cinnamon. Papers on the table visit the porch. Without a barricade,
there is no comfort, only surprise. When a person says yes or no

the answer isn't permanent. The answer opens
a bag full of leaves and broken branches. The answer wraps you

in a hungry kiss and leans against your open frame.

She spreads the photographs of their first years

                                                      together across the floor. He climbs

                     a sand dune, she throws

           fall leaves, they

                   make gingerbread, take naps, wave

             patches of sunlight

                         so glossy and young.

    She runs

                 into water and his arms touch

        sky. Trees

move through seasons and wild animals

                                  peek from corners in nights so dark

              nothing is visible except the flash of captured eyes

She needs a little boy for her lap. One sticky with chocolate who refuses a wash, who pokes her with his elbow as he wiggles his first loose tooth.

A boy small enough for a blanket covered with stars and crescent moons. Who warms and wonders as his face nuzzles her chest.

A boy so big she cannot contain him. With arms that spill from her arms into other planets. With legs that stretch and bend through cosmic dust.

Little boy, she'd whisper if she could reach his ear. *My love. My galaxy. Do what you do.*

The directions on the pass say she can go anywhere the bus goes as many times as she likes forever. She steps aboard and worries that the pass will not work, that the driver will tell her she can't go. But it validates in the electronics and the driver says, "Good morning."

The people on the bus look like they know what they're doing. They reach a station and the woman follows a pretty girl in a peacock-colored coat into the restroom. The girl takes a little black dog out of a bag. The woman watches her feed it. Fingers against the dog's dribbling tongue and slick points of teeth.

The woman boards another bus. The next driver says, "Good afternoon." There is an older man with a pocket watch and a teenager with earphones. In between them—

                    a faint ticking.

She shall soon find a way. Gingerbread after an exile. After the funeral pyre has
    smoked down and the last bread crumbs stolen. How sweet now to have
    found this forest

house, ground cinnamon and ginger, spiced bark and root, a revival. Of course she
    eats it. Life belongs to whoever can find it, to whoever

keeps walking and trying. Children know this. That eating one door leads to
    another. That when captured…

She grabs a handful of gingerbread cake, lines her pockets with crispy cookies,
    licks icing along a window. She is what she does. She is

                                   a molasses-dark shape in the trees.

She walks deep into an unfamiliar park without a map and squints through the morning sun.

Everything moves. Trees branch and leave. Fawns dapple. Wilds flower. She hopes this can continue forever, alone but in company. People chat in many languages and go different ways. Children and old men. Ageless women. What she chooses is what is given. Even God is happy.

In her only dream of him he resurrects Jesus-like
in an airport terminal. "Happy birthday," he whispers.

She runs into the dark cave of his arms and refuses
another separation.

Remember when you were born? he asks over the wheeze of an intercom announcement.
You were born, he promises as travelers pull their luggage past. He hands her

a small, glittering box. *Make sure to remember.*

    This candle—

        beeswax and braided cotton

                A hive. A tree

                Late harvest bees

                        —This candle

        wind   breath

              house

She lives to another spring and follows a trail into the woods.
Two broken trees lean against one another

as if they still hope to grow
as if they knew she needed them.

They form a house and wind opens and shuts the windows. A house
visited by woodpeckers and black crows.

A most generous habitation. So large she cannot remember the door.
So large that when she falls miles and years away, she will still be inside—

All things break and fall against this life,
and this life gathers the shards and makes song.

He returns from the dead so they can discuss Bob Dylan who won the Nobel Prize for literature. People are in an uproar. Should a man doing one thing be recognized for another? He removes his long trench coat that makes him look like a detective and pours himself a glass of milk. What he says always interests her. Dylan's entrance into the Civil Rights movement with "Like a Rolling Stone" and exit from the folk music scene after playing it electric. The time Dylan joined The Band to collaborate. His hand drifts to hers and his eyes are oak branches in water. "My love," he says, "nothing is ever one thing."

They recall the 1998 Bob Dylan/Joni Mitchell show when Joni bitched out two guys standing in front of the stage who weren't listening "I'm a real person up here," she said, "not a fucking t.v." The song before that he swayed behind her, hands cupped against her hips, the closest he ever got to dancing. She looped *Blood on the Tracks* the week she watered his houseplants and when he returned, they scattered pillows on the floor and watched *Don't Look Back*.

He says, "I can't stop touching you," and scoots closer

                                                vibrations in the carpet

                                                             a vanilla-scented candle

notes across the side of her neck as he brushes her hair away

Acknowledgements

Deepest gratitude to Danielle LaVaque-Manty, Jennifer Solheim, and David Ward whose love, kindness, and insight helped me write this book from beginning to end. Scott Beal, Joseph Chapman, Raymond McDaniel, Sean Thomas Dougherty, and Megan Levad encouraged and provided new possibilities. Aimee Nezhukumatathil gave me new forms, and Marianne Boruch's words and teachings continue to guide me.

Ambrose was thrust on this journey with me and bestowed me with a kingdom and a sword. May everyone have them in times of need.

Grateful acknowledgment to the editors of the following publications where these poems were published, sometimes in different forms: *Bateau* ("The Cough"), *december magazine* ("Valentine from the Dead," Snow Continues," "Valentine to the Dead," "Her Only Dream of Him," and "She Lives to Early Spring"), *Gargoyle* ("The Reluctant Hostess"), *Harpur Palate* ("The First Call"), *Honey Pot: A Journal of Intersectional Feminism* ("The Roster" and "Route"), *Plume* ("How to Remove Concrete"), *Weave* ("Pandora," and "She Shall Soon Find a Way"), *Western Humanities Review* ("Sundown" and "Rules for Rearrangement")

"Rules for Rearrangement" and "She Shall Soon Find a Way" appear in the anthology *New Poetry from the Midwest 2017*. "She Shall Soon Find a Way" is also forthcoming in the anthology *Waves: A Confluence of Women's Voices*. Several sections of "Guide" are erasures from an old booklet poet Marianne Boruch put together to welcome MFA students to the area.

About the Author

Julie Babcock is the author of the poetry collection *Autoplay* (MG Press, 2014). Her poetry, fiction, and hybrid writing appear in journals and anthologies including *The Rumpus, Split Lip Magazine,* and *New Poetry from the Midwest (2017)*. She teaches writing in an interdisciplinary program at the University of Michigan and is currently at work on a novel.

Glass Lyre Press

exceptional works to replenish the spirit

Glass Lyre Press is an independent literary publisher interested in technically accomplished, stylistically distinct, and original work. Glass Lyre seeks diverse writers that possess a dynamic aesthetic and an ability to emotionally and intellectually engage a wide audience of readers.

Glass Lyre's vision is to connect the world through language and art. We hope to expand the scope of poetry and short fiction for the general reader through exceptionally well-written books, which evoke emotion, provide insight, and resonate with the human spirit.

Poetry Collections
Poetry Chapbooks
Select Short & Flash Fiction
Anthologies

www.GlassLyrePress.com

www.ingramcontent.com/pod-product-compliance
Lightning Source LLC
Chambersburg PA
CBHW030347100526
44592CB00010B/859